Leaving
a
Legacy

The Journey Study Series

Leaving

a

Legacy

A Thomas Nelson Study Series
Based on *The Journey*
by
BILLY GRAHAM

THOMAS NELSON
Since 1798

NASHVILLE   DALLAS   MEXICO CITY   RIO DE JANEIRO   BEIJING

Published in Nashville, Tennessee. Thomas Nelson is a trademark of Thomas Nelson, Inc.

Thomas Nelson, Inc., titles may be purchased in bulk for educational, business, fund-raising, or sales promotional use. For information, please e-mail SpecialMarkets@ThomasNelson.com.

Leaving a Legacy: A Thomas Nelson Study Series Based on The Journey *by Billy Graham*

ISBN-13: 978-1-4185-1769-4
ISBN-10: 1-4185-1769-0

Printed in the United States of America

07 08 09 10 11 RRD 5 4 3 2 1

Contents

1

The
Family

T O GET THE MOST FROM THIS STUDY GUIDE, READ
pages 267–276 of *The Journey.*

*Parenting is the most important responsibility most of
us will ever face, and none of us does it perfectly.*
BILLY GRAHAM
The Journey

THINK ABOUT IT

*Other things may change us, but we start and end with
family.*

—ANTHONY BRANDT[1]

Sons are a heritage from the LORD,
children a reward from him.

—PSALM 127:3

The family, as we have traditionally defined it, is under attack. Many well-meaning adults are so focused on their jobs and other interests that their families get virtually no attention. Children are left to raise themselves. Parents expect the school system to discipline their children while they attend to their own personal needs and desires.

Other parents take seriously their parental responsibilities. They juggle complex schedules and demands, all in an attempt to live up to God's expectations. They know that their family's future is dependent upon their parental effectiveness. They know parenting is hard, but they know they have no other choice.

REWIND

Briefly describe the hopes and dreams you have for the future generations of your family (your children or other younger relatives, if you have no children).

_____

_____

_____

How much time do you spend each day in direct interaction with other family members?

____ Less than 10 minutes

____ 10 to 30 minutes

____ 30 minutes to 1 hour

____ More than 1 hour

What are the three daily responsibilities that take up the largest portion of your available time?

1. _____

2. _____

3. _____

Children are a gift from God; they are not our personal property. Eventually, our children marry and have children of their own. Children become parents who raise children. Therefore, how you interact with your children today will affect them and future generations. There's a lot riding on your parenting skills.

Read Genesis 33:5. To whom do our children really belong?

_____ Parents

_____ God

Like everything else in life, children are God's property, entrusted to us to raise and train. They are resources that are to be invested for God's purposes. It's not our job to raise doctors, dentists, schoolteachers, homemakers, mechanics, entertainers, and so forth. It is our job to raise children who give their lives to God and commit their lives in service to Him. Then God will guide them into the professions for which He has created them.

JOURNEY THROUGH GOD'S WORD

What is a family? From the biblical viewpoint, it is people who are connected by marriage, genetics, or adoption. In addition, it is the bedrock of human society. In Jacob's family there were three different levels of relationships. The largest was the tribe, then the clan, and finally the family. The family unit was the basic structure in Israel, but the families looked a bit different than they do today.

Many times, multiple generations lived on the same land under the leadership of the elder family head (some-

---

times called a *patriarch*). In communities, the patriarchs might have been the "elders" who were in charge of regulating inter-family disputes. The Bible does, however, make repeated references to the parent-child relationship that we consider the nuclear family.

In the Old Testament, the basis of the family unit was the married couple (Genesis 2:4–5:2). The union of the husband and wife tied together grandparents and grandchildren. The father was responsible for the religious and moral training of the family members (Deuteronomy 6:7, 20–25). In Israelite culture, the wife was not the property of the husband. This was different from the practices of other cultures in the region. The wives gave birth, but the leadership in the home was the role of the husband. Children were taught to respect their parents and to listen to instruction.

In the New Testament, the family was the basic unit through which the early church was established. Individuals who were selected to lead the church first had to prove themselves as leaders of their homes. Ephesians 5–6 and Colossians 3–4 contain Paul's words regarding the family. In the Bible, wives are described as the household administrators; therefore, family decisions should be made with the wife's input.[2]

As you can see, the family was the core of biblical societies. The same should be true today! Read 2 Timothy 3:2–3. When the family is destroyed, society disintegrates.

RETHINK

Think back on your childhood. Place an X on the line, indicating the spiritual strength of your family.

Very Weak -- Very Strong

What about your present family? Place a Y on the line, indicating the spiritual strength of your immediate family.

What is your goal? Place a Z on the line, representing the spiritual strength you would like to see in your family.

Explain the differences between X and Y. Is your present family spiritually stronger or weaker than the family in which you were raised? Why?

_____

_____

_____

What are you doing to achieve your spiritual goals for your immediate family? Are you making satisfactory progress? Why or why not?

_____

_____

_____

_____

It is easy to get so focused on our personal needs and wants that we inadvertently ignore other family members—especially our children. It happens to almost every parent.

What are some personal activities that eat away at the time you have available for other people?

_____

_____

_____

_____

REFLECT

> *If you have children, never lose sight of the fact that God gave them to you. Our children are a gift from God, and someday we must give an account to Him for the way we raised them. For the Christian, family life isn't a detour; it's an important part of our discipleship.*
> BILLY GRAHAM
> *The Journey*

Why does God give us children? There are many reasons besides the obvious reason that the continuation of the human race depends upon the continuation of the human life cycle. Here are a few additional reasons God gives us children.

1. **God gives us children so we can prepare them to become adults.**

   This sounds simple, but it is a complex process. For one thing, we have to ensure their physical safety. Today's news often features tragic stories about child abduction or abuse. It is our responsibility to do everything possible to prevent such things from happening. Even then, there are no guarantees, but we must try.

2. **God gives us children to help them develop mentally and emotionally.**

   Physical development of our children is important, but their mental and emotional development is equally important.

Read Luke 2:52. What were the three types of growth Jesus experienced?

_____

_____

_____

How are you training your children in these areas?

_____

_____

_____

3. **God gives us children so we can shape their moral and spiritual character.**

   We can't help but wonder what will come of the moral fabric of our society. Recent history has given us reason to be concerned about the future. Many people—even some professed Christians—no longer believe in absolute moral standards. Yet a biblical foundation is critical to these areas of development.

Read Matthew 7:24–27. What is the danger of a weak moral and spiritual foundation?

_____

_____

_____

_____

How are you teaching morality and spirituality to your children?

_____

_____

_____

_____

We can't force our children to believe like we do; we must provide the environment for moral and spiritual growth.

Read Deuteronomy 11:19. What is the parental responsibility described in this verse?

_____

_____

_____

What are the sources from which our children (and many adults) get their moral boundaries?

_____ Musicians

_____ Athletes

_____ Friends

_____ Celebrities

_____ News media

_____ The Bible

_____ Parents

_____ Other: _____

But how do you become a wise parent? Like everything else, it is a process that requires you to know what to do, and it requires you to make the commitment to keep doing it. You can't be a wise parent one day and decide it's not worth the trouble the next. Here are four things you can do.

1. **Commit your family to God.**

   Raising children requires godly wisdom, and godly wisdom is found through a personal relationship with God. The Bible teaches discipline, responsibility, interpersonal relationships, and more. However, the Bible does not address every possible situation verbatim. Instead it offers principles that can be applied to most every situation, including the situations within a family.

Match the following Scriptures with their primary messages regarding parental responsibilities:

_____ Deuteronomy 6:7	a. To nurture
_____ Proverbs 22:6	b. To control
_____ 2 Corinthians 12:14	c. To train
_____ Ephesians 6:4	d. To teach
_____ 1 Timothy 3:4	e. To love
_____ Titus 2:4	f. To provide for

Answers are found at the end of this chapter.

Every situation you face falls into one of the categories above. Therefore, parents must look for opportunities that give them the opportunity to nurture, control, train, and so forth. Through words and actions, parents teach children about God.

Through your interactions with them, what are you teaching your children about God?

_____

_____

_____

_____

_____

_____

2. **Give priority to your family.**

   There are plenty of things demanding your attention. How do you decide what gets the most of your time? Are you making the effort to make your children feel special?

With whom of the following do your children spend a significant amount of time?

_____ Parents

_____ Siblings

_____ Grandparents

_____ Aunts and uncles

_____ Godparents

_____ Other: _____

Are you comfortable with the spiritual influence each of the above exerts on your children?

_____ Yes   _____ No   _____ Sometimes

How should you handle negative influences on your children?

_____

_____

_____

_____

3. **Put love at the center of your family.**
   Everyone needs to know he or she is loved—including children. Love doesn't mean giving in to their wants. Sometimes it means saying no or enforcing the rules.

Read Proverbs 19:18. What is the primary message of this verse?

_____

_____

_____

What does Proverbs 29:15, 17 say about raising children?

_____

_____

_____

Throughout Scripture, we are reminded that love is our primary responsibility. We are told to love God and love each other. Love isn't always used in the romantic sense. The Greek language has different words for each kind of love. Love for

God is due Him because He is the Creator and Provider. Love for each other is the mutual respect due God's creation. Love for children is the guiding responsibility we have for those God entrusts to our care.

In a world that is often so void of love, our homes need to be places where God's love ripples through everything we do.

4. Keep the door open.

The parenting relationship doesn't end when your children move out. You might discover that your children need you more after they become adults. Keep the door open, and let your relationship adjust to that of adult to adult rather than parent to child.

Some children will leave home in rebellion. Pray for them and do everything you can to bring them back to God. In doing so, you'll bring them back into a right relationship with you.

Read Isaiah 32:2. What would it take for this verse to be true of your home?

_____

_____

_____

Maybe you are looking back and seeing some mistakes you made along the way. The bad news is that you can't go back and undo them. The good news is that God can give you and your family a fresh start. Begin now by putting past failures behind you and looking forward to what God will do in the future. Begin each day with a commitment of your family to God, and you might be surprised at what He will do.

REACT

No matter where you are in the child-raising process, God has a message for you. If you don't have children yet, this is a great time to begin making preparations just in case God chooses to bless you in that way. If you already have children, you can become a more godly influence on them no matter how young or old they are. Reflect on what God has said to you in this study.

Our children should grow up feeling they are special, but it won't happen if we are too busy. Sometimes we need to stop and ask ourselves, "How will my children remember their childhood? Will their memories be of fun and happiness? Or will they be resentful because I didn't make time for them?"

BILLY GRAHAM
The Journey

What are three truths you learned in this study, and how will you apply each truth to your daily life?

1. _____

_____

_____

_____

_____

2. _____

_____

_____

_____

_____

3. _____

_____

_____

_____

_____

_____

Answers to Scripture matching on page 14 —

Deuteronomy 6:7 (d); Proverbs 22:6 (c); 2 Corinthians 12:14 (f);
Ephesians 6:4 (a); 1 Timothy 3:4 (b); Titus 2:4 (e)

2

Making
an
Impact

T O GET THE MOST FROM THIS STUDY GUIDE, READ
pages 277–286 of *The Journey*.

---

*Earth isn't just heaven's waiting room, where we sit
around doing nothing until it's finally time for us to
depart. Earth is the stage on which the drama of the ages
is being played out—the drama of Christ's victory over
sin and death and hell and Satan. And no matter who
we are, we have a God-given role to play in that divine
drama.*

BILLY GRAHAM
The Journey

THINK ABOUT IT

What you want to do, you do. The rest is just talk.

—JOHN CLEEK[1]

You are the light of the world. . . . Let your light shine before men, that they may see your good deeds and praise your Father in heaven.

—Matthew 5:14, 16

Why doesn't God just take us to heaven the moment we are saved? Because He has something for us to do. Our ultimate destination is heaven, but while we are on earth, there is much to be done. If God didn't have something for us to do, He wouldn't have left us here.

So, why are so many Christians not making a difference in the world? Because they choose not to make a difference. The quote on the previous page is right; you do what you want to do. If you want to make a difference for God, you will do those things that matter to Him. If you don't make a difference for Him, it's because you haven't chosen the actions that are important to God.

REWIND

What are some things you intentionally do that make a positive impact for God on those around you?

_____

_____

_____

What are some of the excuses you've used to avoid making an impact for God?

_____ I don't know what to say.

_____ I don't have time.

_____ I'm afraid they'll ask me a question I can't answer.

_____ There are others much more qualified to do this.

_____ Other:_____

What are some other difficult activities that you do on a regular basis?

_____

_____

_____

God has an assignment for you. Since He is the owner of everything that exists, He has the right to determine how His property is used. There are two jobs that are universal—honoring God and telling others the good news of Jesus Christ. Your vocation is the vehicle through which God allows you to do these two things. Your vocation isn't your life!

Read John 15:8. What is it that brings glory to God?

____ **Acting religious**

____ **Bearing spiritual fruit**

____ **Being a church leader**

____ **Being successful in your job**

Bearing spiritual fruit is simply making a difference for God everywhere you go. It sounds easy, but it can be a challenge. Think about times when your patience is tried. Are you making a difference for God in those situations? What about when things don't go your way at work? How about when your children misbehave? It's tough to stay spiritually sharp in a world that tends to dull our spiritual senses.

JOURNEY THROUGH GOD'S WORD

Early in the Bible, we hear God say, "Let there be light" (Genesis 1:3). With that command, light became a symbol of God's presence and power in the world and in the lives

---

of those who know Him. In the Old Testament, light represents the following:

1. Instruction (Isaiah 2:5; Psalm 119:105, 130)

2. Truth (Psalm 43:3)

3. Good (Isaiah 5:20)

4. Salvation (Psalm 27:1)

5. Life (Job 33:28–30)

6. Peace (Isaiah 45:7)

7. Rejoicing (Psalm 97:11)

8. Covenant (Isaiah 42:6)

9. Justice and righteousness (Isaiah 59:9)

10. God's presence and favor (Psalm 89:15)

11. The glory of God (Isaiah 60:1–3)[2]

All of the references above are connected to God's character, which explains why light and dark are set as opposites representing good and evil, respectively. The absence of God's character is the breeding ground for sin and evil. Where God's character is evident, there can be no darkness.

In Matthew 5:14–16, Jesus identified His followers as the "light of the world." The implication is that Christians are to let God's character shine in their lives so that those who see them will see God and be drawn to Him. That's a tremendous challenge for today's Christians.

RETHINK

Reflect on your spiritual journey. What are three situations that made a dramatic impact on your spiritual life?

1. _____

_____

_____

_____

2. _____

_____

_____

_____

3. _____

_____

_____

_____

What are three situations in which God has worked through you to make a spiritual impact on someone else?

1. _____

_____

_____

_____

2. _____

_____

_____

_____

3. _____

_____

_____

_____

Which was the easiest list to recount? Why?

_____

_____

_____

Think about a football team with a valued place kicker. The game is on the line, and the team is down by two points. After driving down the field, the team is in position to kick the winning field goal. The place kicker is on the team for this purpose. Yet, when the coach calls on him to enter the game, the kicker declines, saying he prefers the warmth of the team bench to the joy of doing his job. Ridiculous, right?

But the same situation is repeated daily in the lives of Christians who have a God-designed job to do but who choose to sit on the bench and allow others to struggle with responsibilities that aren't theirs. God equips His church to do its work, yet much work goes undone because God's people refuse to do those things for which they were designed.

When it comes to your God-given responsibilities, which are you?

_____ A benchwarmer who is letting others do your job

_____ A team player who is making a contribution

REFLECT

So, why did God leave you here? Wouldn't you love to discover the answer to that question? It's impossible to uncover the specifics of your assignment from God, but we can take a look at Scripture and discover the general boundaries of the calling of all believers. *The overarching calling for all believers is to bring honor and glory to God in the way that we live.* This calling governs all other activities in life.

Read Ephesians 1:4, 12. What do these verses say about the lives of believers?

_____

_____

_____

> *The Bible compares us to salt, lamps, yeast, and seed—none of which is of any use as long as it's kept in a closed container. Doing so might preserve them—but that isn't their purpose. So too with us. How can we remain silent and unconcerned, bottling up the Gospel instead of sharing it with others? To do so is to miss God's purpose in keeping us here.*
>
> BILLY GRAHAM
> *The Journey*

Honoring God is the governing principle, but how do we do it? First, we must tell other people the good news of Christ.

Read 1 Peter 2:9 and Mark 16:15. Do these verses apply to you?

____ Yes   ____ No (if so, explain)

_____

_____

_____

What are some things you do on a regular basis to fulfill this responsibility?

_____

_____

_____

Who are some people who have shown God's love to you through the way they live their lives?

_____

_____

_____

We can agree that we are supposed to glorify God by showing His love to the world around us. But how can we do that? What can we change in our lives so that we will be more in tune with God's purposes for us?

1. **Ask God to help you see the world the way He sees it.**

   Hurting people are everywhere, and God brings certain people across your path in order to give you the opportunity to show His love to them.

Why don't we see people the way God sees them?

_____ We don't care about others.

_____ We don't know how God sees them.

_____ We are only concerned about ourselves.

_____ All of the above.

Read 2 Corinthians 5:14–16. How does your view of the world compare to Paul's statement?

_____

_____

_____

2. **Demonstrate Christ's love by the way you live.**
   If you are a Christian, your life is a statement about God—but is the statement being made by your life accurate? Too many non-believers blame their lack of faith on the actions of so-called followers of Christ. We don't have to look far to find examples of such behavior. You can't control how others act, but you are responsible for yourself.

Read Matthew 18:6. What is Jesus' warning regarding causing someone else to stumble?

_____

_____

_____

_____

Read Romans 14:12–13. What is the point of Paul's statement in these verses?

_____

_____

_____

_____

Jesus highlighted the simple ways of showing God's love to other people. In Matthew 10:42, a cup of cold water offered to a thirsty person is an example of showing God's love.

What are some "cup of cold water" things you can do for those around you?

_____

_____

_____

_____

3. **Learn to share your faith with others.**

Doing nice things is no substitute for telling people about God. When you meet someone's needs, that person may conclude that you are a very nice person. But that person will never conclude anything about God unless you speak up.

For many Christians, sharing their faith is something they just can't seem to do. Why? For one thing, many people have assumed that canned or packaged presentations are the only "approved" ways to share one's faith. However, the most effective means aren't found in memorizing an outline or key questions. Believers are most effective when they simply share with others what God is doing in their lives.

Read Romans 10:14. What are you doing to communicate God's message with those you encounter?

_____

_____

_____

What are three things God is doing in your life right now?

1. _____

_____

_____

_____

2. _____

_____

_____

_____

3. _____

_____

_____

_____

What are three things God has done for you in the past month?

1. _____

_____

_____

_____

2. _____

_____

_____

_____

3. _____

_____

_____

_____

There are four main points that should be made when talking with others about God's love for them. Commit to memory these points and the related Scripture passages.

a. *God created us, loves us, and wants us to live at peace with Him forever (Genesis 2:7; John 10:10).*

b. *We all have sinned and turned away from God, and as a result we are cut off from Him and subject to His judgment (Romans 3:23; Isaiah 59:2).*

c. *God still loves us, and He sent His only Son, Jesus Christ, into the world to take the judgment we deserve and bring us back to God (Romans 5:8; Romans 6:23; 1 Peter 3:18).*

d. *We must respond in faith by trusting Jesus Christ as our Savior and committing our lives to Him as Lord (John 3:16; John 1:12; Romans 10:9).*

Write these notes in the back of your Bible, and use your daily quiet time to meditate on the Scripture passages so that you can explain them to people in your own words.

When should you be prepared to share your faith? Take a look at Peter's words in 1 Peter 3:15.

_____

_____

_____

Remember, only God can change someone's heart. We are responsible for presenting God's love, praying, and encouraging, but you and I cannot save anyone. When a person rejects the message of God, that person is rejecting God, not you or me.

4. **Pray for the opportunity to share God's love with others and for the willingness of others to hear God's voice.**

Read Colossians 4:3. Paul understood the importance of assembling prayer partners in ministry. You need prayer part-

ners, too. List three people who might partner with you in prayer for the unsaved people God has placed in your life.

1. _____

2. _____

3. _____

The open door of opportunity is the work of the Holy Spirit. When people are willing to hear you talk about God, it is only because God already has been at work preparing those people to listen.

REACT

What should you do in response to this lesson? You can choose to ignore it and miss out on the blessing of being used by God to change your world. You can choose to agree but do nothing about your agreement. If you do that, you will also miss God's blessing in your life. The only other choice is to step up and say, "Use me, Lord, to make an impact on the world." That's a scary thought, but God will lead you every step of the way. Jesus needed workers in the early days of His ministry. Workers still are needed today.

Read Luke 10:2. What is your response to this verse?

_____ Let someone else do it.

_____ I'll do it!

There are no other options. You can choose obedience and the joy that accompanies it, or you can choose disobedience and the spiritual frustration that accompanies it. When it comes to making a difference for God, your life can be radically changed by asking yourself one question before you make any decision: *Will doing this bring glory and honor to God?* If the answer is yes, proceed. But if the answer is no, stop! God never calls His children to do anything that will disappoint Him.

Pray for those around you who do not know Christ. You cannot pray consistently for someone to come to Christ but remain indifferent to them. Nor can you pray for their salvation without realizing that God may want to use you to touch their lives. Before prayer changes others, it first changes us.

BILLY GRAHAM
The Journey

What are three truths you learned in this study, and how will you apply each truth to your daily life?

1. _____

_____

_____

_____

2. _____

_____

_____

_____

3. _____

_____

_____

_____

3

As
Life Moves
On

T O GET THE MOST FROM THIS STUDY GUIDE, READ
pages 287–292 of *The Journey.*

It's not only how you start a race that's important, but how you finish—and the same is true of the Christian life. Nor do we have the option of finishing it or not finishing it; the journey continues as long as we live. The only question is, how will we finish?

BILLY GRAHAM
The Journey

THINK ABOUT IT

I cannot conceive of getting old. I have a life that is never going to end.

—DWIGHT L. MOODY[1]

Even to your old age and gray hairs
I am he, I am he who will sustain you.
I have made you and I will carry you;
I will sustain you and I will rescue you.

—ISAIAH 46:4

There is a growing interest in running marathons. People who run them suggest that a potential marathon runner spend time in training because the race is more about endurance and finishing strong than jumping out to an early lead.

Our marriages can be that way. We start strong and do well, but a lack of training and discipline costs us years later. When we approach those adult years when our family makeup changes and our awareness of our age increases, we need to be prepared. What we do today will affect how we handle life later.

Our Christian lives are much the same. Starting fast is easy, but maintaining a healthy pace for the long haul can be a problem. Don't misunderstand; once you accept Jesus Christ as your Lord and Savior, your salvation is secure. That's not what we're talking about. This is all about continuing to make maturing in our faith a priority. Some people will choose to finish strongly; others will limp to the finish. You will finish the race, but how?

REWIND

Think back over your adult life. If possible, note some of the spiritual highs and lows of your journey.

_____

_____

_____

How would you describe your spiritual journey?

_____ A series of very high highs and very low lows

_____ A series of highs and lows, but overall strengthening

_____ A series of highs and lows, but overall weakening

_____ Only highs

We are on a journey that continues throughout our lives. This journey will have its ups and downs and will be stressful at times. How we handle the journey is important, but more important is how we finish the journey.

Israel's King Saul is an interesting study because his life parallels the lives of many people who begin strong and finish weak. Saul began with a keen awareness of God's presence in his life. He credited God with the victories and sought God's guidance in his decisions. Yet, at the end of his life, Saul was a desperate man. His commitment to God had been long forgotten and he was on a mission to murder David, the man God selected to become the new king of Israel. What happened to Saul? We aren't sure, but we do see that his initial desire to please God eventually was replaced by a desire for self-gratification. One thing led to another and, at the end of his life, Saul was nothing like he was when we first encountered him.

Is your life anything like Saul's life? Describe the things you do to keep from following in Saul's footsteps.

_____

_____

_____

JOURNEY THROUGH GOD'S WORD

Saul was the first king of Israel following the period of the judges. He was anointed by Samuel and faced some skepticism. However, he proved himself to be a capable military leader. He reigned for approximately twenty years and operated from a modest fortress near Jerusalem.

He had encounters with the Philistines and other enemies of Israel. His commitment to and dependence upon God, however, began to slip, and he made some serious spiritual mistakes that eventually led to his being rejected by God (1 Samuel 15:7–23). When God's Spirit departed Saul, an evil spirit took over. It was during his torment by the evil spirit that David soothed him by playing the lyre (1 Samuel 16:14–23).

Saul was in command when the Israelites faced off against Goliath and the Philistines. After defeating Goliath and driving the Philistines out of the area, David became a folk hero. This was something that Saul just couldn't handle.

David became a man on the run as Saul grew more and more desperate to eliminate him. He murdered the priests at Nob (1 Samuel 22:17–19) and consulted the witch at Endor (1 Samuel 28:7–8) before being killed (along with three of his sons) in battle on the following day.[2]

Saul presents a classic example of what happens when one's ego begins to control his or her life. Saul abandoned the very thing that had been his source of success, believing that he could go his own way and allow

God into his life on an "as-needed" basis. In the end, his self-sufficiency was his undoing. Saul's life serves as a good reminder that we all must continually express our dependence on God and remind ourselves that, apart from God's grace, we can do nothing.

RETHINK

As you look ahead, what are the most significant challenges to your spiritual growth?

_____ Career

_____ Hobbies

_____ Finances

_____ Possessions

_____ Family

_____ Past failure

_____ Addictions

_____ Other: _____

What can you do to spiritually strengthen yourself against these threats?

_____

_____

_____

_____

> *Every stage of life has its own temptations and dangers, and Satan will do all he can to exploit them. As we grow older, we may not face the same temptations we did when we were young—but we will still be tempted. And because they may be different from those we experienced before, they can catch us off guard.*
>
> BILLY GRAHAM
> *The Journey*

Life is a series of significant events, both in your life and in the lives of those you love. From the early days of adulthood to the latter stages of life, we all are on the same journey. Some of us are just beginning while others are nearing the end of our days on earth. Every stage of life has its challenges and temptations.

Consider the following decades. What do you think are the most significant challenges facing adults in these years?

Twenties:

_____

_____

_____

Thirties:

_____

_____

_____

Forties:

_____

_____

_____

Fifties:

_____

_____

_____

Sixties:

_____

_____

_____

Seventies and beyond:

_____

_____

_____

In the next lesson, we'll take a look at the retirement years and how to prepare for them and find fulfillment them. For now, we need to consider how we can mature so that we become spiritually stronger with each passing decade.

REFLECT

The stages of life present unique challenges for each of us. Aging is a natural process that brings about changes in the way we work, relate, and serve God. One of the things that we all will face one day (if we have children) is an empty nest.

We spend much of our adult lives preparing for the day when we will launch our children into living on their own. It's a bittersweet moment of sadness and accomplishment. Making it through this time of change presents another set of challenges.

Beware of marital discord. Some couples confess to staying together for the sake of their children. If your marital relationship is built only around your children, you will struggle when the children are gone.

What are some things you can do to improve your marriage before you get to the empty-nest years?

_____

_____

_____

Before it's too late, consider some of these activities.

- Have a regularly scheduled "date night" each week in which you get a sitter and spend time with your spouse. Don't talk about the kids or work; talk about your relationship and hopes and dreams for the future.

- At least once each year, get away together for a weekend alone. Do things that interest both of you and leave the kids with someone you can trust so you won't worry about them.

- Make ordinary days special by sending flowers, cooking a special meal, playing games together, and so forth. Don't wait for special occasions to have special days.

- Minimize the time you spend doing what you want to do, and maximize the time you spend doing what you both want to do. Many couples develop deep interests in things that don't involve the other spouse. Though those things may be good, they can become a distraction if taken to the extreme.

Read the following Scriptures and summarize what each says about marriage:

Genesis 2:24

_____

_____

_____

Matthew 5:32

_____

_____

_____

Mark 10:9

_____

_____

_____

How would you summarize God's view of marriage?

_____

_____

_____

Don't become preoccupied with other things. In our multifaceted lives, it is easy to become preoccupied with any one of a number of important matters.

What are some facets of life with which you could easily become preoccupied?

_____

_____

_____

What are some things you can do to keep that from happening?

_____

_____

_____

First Corinthians 13 is well known as the "love chapter" because of Paul's articulate description of love and its supreme value in life. Nearing the end of that chapter, Paul interjects his comments about spiritual childhood and spiritual adulthood. Think for a moment about the characteristics of a young child—self-aware, unconcerned about you and your schedule, demanding, and so forth. The sad fact is that many seasoned Christians still exhibit these qualities in their spiritual lives. Spiritual maturity has nothing to do with how long you've been a Christian; it is a by-product of authentic spiritual growth that happens as followers of Christ invest themselves in studying God's Word and growing closer to Him in community with other believers and in prayer. When it comes to our marriage relationships, we must all seek spiritual maturity and not remain spiritual children.

Protect your relationship with God. In the busyness of life, it is easy to push God to the edges and make spending time with Him an optional activity. When this happens, life begins to change.

Read 1 Samuel 9:17; 1 Samuel 13:13–14; 1 Samuel 15:10–11; and 1 Samuel 15:24–29. Briefly describe the spiritual change in Saul's life.

_____

_____

_____

What are some things you can do to keep something similar from happening in your life?

_____

_____

_____

_____

REACT

It's easy to grow older without maturing spiritually. That's why there are so many seasoned Christians who have no spiritual power in their lives. They have allowed themselves to become bored with the spiritual baby food that has been their primary diet, yet they aren't prepared to handle the solid food of God's Word.

That might seem fine when life is going smoothly; but when those transition years hit, and we find ourselves facing an empty nest and the other changes that accompany that stage in life, we need all the spiritual strength we can muster. That's when we need to know what we believe and why we believe it.

It's easy, however, to compromise when it comes to God's Word. We make up our minds to do something with no regard for what God's Word says. That's when our faith and desires conflict, and we are left to make a decision.

How do you respond when God's Word challenges you on a certain thought, behavior, or belief that you hold dear?

_____ I ignore God's Word.

_____ I rationalize my actions.

_____ I reinterpret God's Word to fit what I'm doing.

_____ I change my way of life.

Too many Christians choose something other than the last response. They ignore God's Word and focus only on the "feel good" passages that aren't so confrontational. They use human reasoning to "make sense" out of thoughts and actions that are inconsistent with God's character as revealed in Scripture. They even apply new interpretations to God's Word so that it supports what they've decided to do. Each of these choices is a decision to remain a spiritual baby—obstinate, self-centered, demanding. Why would a non-believer ever want to become one of those?

What are three truths you learned in this study and how will you apply each truth to your daily life?

1. _____

    _____

    _____

    _____

2. _____

    _____

    _____

    _____

3. _____

    _____

    _____

    _____

4

Retirement: A New Beginning

To GET THE MOST FROM THIS STUDY GUIDE, READ pages 293–297 of *The Journey*.

Many people plan financially for retirement—but not spiritually and emotionally. Work isn't only earning a living; work gives us a sense of purpose and worth and opportunities for companionship. But retirement changes this, and many aren't prepared for it.

BILLY GRAHAM
The Journey

THINK ABOUT IT

Some people are born about sixty-five years old and are always ready to retire. Some stay twenty-one until they are ninety.

—SIR WILLIAM BEVERIDGE[1]

Gray hair is a crown of splendor;
it is attained by a righteous life.

—PROVERBS 16:31

Retirement is not common in all cultures of the world. In the American culture, it has become a goal for much of the workforce. People will tolerate all sorts of negative work conditions in hopes that they will receive what has been promised to them throughout their careers.

Today, more and more people dislike their jobs, and employee retention is something that requires the help of high-priced consultants. Work seems to be something many people want to escape. The number of adults returning to college is growing faster than anyone might have imagined. People of all ages are looking for fresh starts in life . . . the same fresh start that retirement provides for those who have reached the appropriate age.

This lesson isn't exclusively for the retired people in our midst. It is for everyone who is looking to make a fresh start in life. Some people might change jobs; others might renew their enthusiasm for the jobs they have. In other words, this lesson is for you!

REWIND

What is the first thought that comes to mind when you think about retirement?

_____

_____

_____

If *retirement* was eliminated from the dictionary, what other word or phrase would you use to describe the concept?

_____

_____

_____

Work was not the curse pronounced on Adam when he and Eve sinned in the Garden of Eden. In Genesis 2:15—before the Fall—the Bible says that man was placed in the garden to "tend it and keep it." In Genesis 3:17–19, the ground was cursed because of the man's sin, and work was made more difficult. Man was created to have meaningful work that honors and pleases God.

How does the concept of retirement compare to Genesis 2:15 and 3:17–19?

_____

_____

_____

Journey through God's Word

We often refer to those who are older than us as our "elders." The term has a certain modern meaning, but that meaning is far-removed from the biblical meaning of the word.

In biblical times, elders were prominent members of the faith community. In Old Testament times, the term translated as *elder* comes from the root word referring to "the beard" or "the chin." In the New Testament, the term is connected to the family of terms that eventually was translated as *priest*.

In the Old Testament, the elders were leaders of different tribes. The formation of the nation of Israel elevated the leaders to national prominence. The Bible points to the fact that elders were present in Israel before Moses delivered them from Egyptian captivity (Exodus 3:16ff). As the nation grew, the leadership was diversified and the elders took on a political role in addition to their religious responsibilities.

Throughout the Old Testament, the elders were key players in the appointment of Saul as king (1 Samuel 8:4–5), David's ascension to the throne (2 Samuel 3:17; 5:3), and the consecration of Solomon's temple (1 Kings 8:1–3). The elders also served judicial roles in cases involving the family and community decisions.

In the New Testament, the elders were affiliated with the synagogue and eventually are associated with the leadership of the early church (Acts 15). Some of the churches had elders who performed pastoral functions, although Paul tended to focus more on the work of the ministry rather than the titles of the ministers.[2]

In today's church, many people believe the "professional ministers" have more responsibilities than other members of the congregation. They expect the ministers to do the work of ministry while they watch. That's one of the problems plaguing today's church.

RETHINK

If you were to retire, what do you think God would want you to do next?

Retirement isn't the end of one's working life; it is the beginning of something new. In many situations, the retirement years provide the opportunity for someone to engage in work without regard for the income it provides.

If money was not an issue, what would you do with your life?

_____

_____

_____

_____

Take a look at your response. Which statement below best characterizes your response?

_____ This is something I want to do for my benefit.

_____ This is something I want to do for the benefit of others.

Many people work looking forward to the day when they can stop working and do something they really want to do. There seems to be an undercurrent that tells us that work is something that can't be enjoyed. Yet many people work with the idea that they will continue doing their jobs until they are physically unable to do it or they choose to stop.

There are countless examples of people beyond their prime who started businesses that grew into successful corporations. "Retired" people have gone on to become artists, authors, inventors, entrepreneurs, teachers, missionaries, tutors, customer service representatives, and everything else you can imagine. Retirement isn't the end; it's a new beginning.

Consider your plans for retirement. In what ways have you planned:

a. Financially?

_____

_____

_____

b. Spiritually?

_____

_____

_____

c. Emotionally?

_____

_____

_____

_____

_____

Work provides us a sense of purpose and worth. In addition, through our work, we develop relationships with people who share common goals and face common challenges. When retirement comes, the support structure that has been associated with work changes. This can lead to people not having anything to do with their time. Therefore, they feel unfulfilled. This can produce a spiritual problem as people question God's plans for their lives. It becomes a never-ending cycle.

God, however, isn't finished with you. As long as you are on His earth, He has a purpose for your life. Christians never retire from their service to God; we simply get the opportunity to serve God in new and exciting ways.

What are some ways you can serve God through:

a. A part-time job?

_____

_____

_____

b. Volunteer work in your community or church?

_____

_____

_____

c. Short-term missions work?

_____

_____

_____

d. Your hobbies?

_____

_____

_____

_____

e. Other opportunities?

_____

_____

_____

_____

Pray, asking God to show you what He would have you do.

REFLECT

From the moment we are born, we are on a collision course with the end of life as we know it. As life progresses, it is normal for us to become more and more aware of our ailments and problems. If we aren't careful, Satan will use these natural processes to make us believe that we are unable to continue to serve God. This is one of Satan's most effective tools against the aging Christian.

Read Matthew 28:20. What did Jesus say about His plans for your life?

_____ He will use us until we reach retirement age and then replace us with a younger person.

_____ He will keep us frustrated and never allow us to see His plans for us.

_____ He will park us on a bench and let us watch life pass us by.

_____ He will be with us until the very end of our days.

Life gives you a variety of opportunities—some good, some not so good. Through all of them, you learn some valuable life lessons that can be used to encourage and teach other Christians. As you approach retirement age, you transition into a different role—a role that puts you in a position to influence younger, less-seasoned believers.

> *Old age is Satan's last chance to blow us off course, however—and you can be sure he'll try. Don't wait until the storms of old age threaten to blow you off course; now is the time to strengthen your faith. The stronger our relationship with Christ, the stronger our defense against the devil's temptations.*
>
> BILLY GRAHAM
> *The Journey*

What can you do to stay on course throughout your life? Here are a few suggestions.

1. **Be alert to the dangers.**

   Later in life, you have had enough experiences to see some problems before they arise. If you read 2 Samuel 11–12, you'll see God's chosen servant, David, fall into sin. This was the chosen king of Israel, the man who would unite the nation and restore God's influence. Yet, in a moment of weakness, he violated the basic tenets of his faith and committed adultery with Bathsheba. Did he know better? Sure! But the temptation was stronger than his relationship with God, so temptation won.

What are the temptations that could derail your spiritual journey?

_____ Money

_____ Possessions

_____ Lust

_____ Laziness

_____ Fame

_____ Ego

_____ Other: _____

What can you do to guard yourself against these temptations?

_____

_____

_____

_____

Read Proverbs 4:23. How can you make this verse a reality in your life?

_____

_____

_____

_____

2. **Strengthen your commitment to Christ.**
   Building your spiritual strength is a task for the present, not the future! A conditional relationship with God weakens you spiritually. God isn't an umbrella for a rainy day; He is a constant source of strength for every day.

Read Proverbs 10:9. How can you develop more integrity?

_____

_____

_____

_____

3. **Commit every situation to God and trust Him for the outcome.**

    Sometimes our prayers are actually requests for God to work things out to our specifications. When we do that, and God doesn't answer our prayers the way we wanted, we doubt our relationship with God. The problems you face are opportunities for God to exhibit His love for you in fresh, new ways.

What are a few of the fears you are facing right now?

_____

_____

_____

On a scale of 1 to 10, with 10 being maximum anxiety, how much anxiety do you have about each of your fears?

_____

_____

_____

_____

Read Isaiah 26:4. What does this verse say to you about the fears you face?

_____

_____

_____

What happens in your life that comes as a surprise to God? Nothing! If He knew you before you were born, He knows what you're going through right now. You haven't been forgotten! God loves you and wants to demonstrate His love on a daily basis. Will you let Him love you?

4. **Strengthen the relationships God already has given you.**

What are the primary relationships in your life, and how strong are they?

Weak   Strong

1   2   3   4   5

_____ Spouse

_____ Children

_____ Friends

_____ Extended family

_____ Fellow believers

What can you do to strengthen each of these relationships?

_____

_____

_____

Satan went to Jesus while He was alone in the desert. Satan attacks you when you are alone. As children grow older, we must transition our support structure to other people, such as fellow believers. You need the support of other believers, and you need to be a support to others.

REACT

How will your life be measured? Will the things that are important to you now be the criteria by which you are evaluated later? Probably not! We spend a lot of our lives pursuing castles, cars, and careers to the exclusion of things that are valuable to God. The pursuit of worldly gain often leaves people empty. So this house is sold, and a bigger, better house is purchased. But the attraction is short-lived.

Read 2 Timothy 4:7. Think of your life into the future. Will this statement by Paul be true of you? Why or why not?

_____

_____

_____

What can you do to make this statement true about you?

_____

_____

_____

Are you on course to finish well? Are you investing your life in things that really matter? Are you putting together a spiritual defense against the attacks of Satan? It's easy to go through the prime of our lives without concern for these issues. Yet, later in life they become big issues. Paul faced incredible difficulties but remained true to God. You, too, will face problems that will require your allegiance to God. Growing in your faith is not an option; it is a life-saving device!

> *Our later years can be the most fulfilling of our lives—*
> *if we commit them to God.*
>
> BILLY GRAHAM
> *The Journey*

What are three truths you learned in this study, and how will you apply each truth to your daily life?

1. _____

   _____

   _____

   _____

2. _____

   _____

   _____

   _____

3. _____

_____

_____

_____

5

Our
Final
Destination

TO GET THE MOST FROM THIS STUDY GUIDE, READ pages 298–302 of *The Journey*.

Sometimes life's harshness comes upon us suddenly and without warning; sometimes it stays with us most of our lives. Life's road is often very rough. Life is hard— but God is good, and heaven is real.

BILLY GRAHAM
The Journey

THINK ABOUT IT

Our destination is home with our Father in heaven. It is so easy on this journey to lose sight of the destination and to focus on the detours of this life instead. This life is only the trip to get home.

—BOB SNYDER[1]

He will wipe every tear from their eyes. There will be no more death or mourning or crying or pain, for the old order of things has passed away.

—Revelation 21:4

Life isn't easy. For many people, their goal is to get through each day without a major issue or problem. The immediacy of today blocks their view of a future with no problems.

A life free from death, mourning, crying, and pain is a universal desire. But people seem to have differing opinions as to how to make it a reality. Ponce de Leon unsuccessfully searched for the Fountain of Youth, and multitudes continue that search today. From infomercials to New Age philosophy, people are convinced that they can achieve an earthly existence that is free from death, pain, and other unpleasant experiences.

The good news is that this kind of life is possible. The bad news is that it isn't possible this side of heaven! You will spend eternity in a real place, and you only have two choices. Will you choose heaven or default to eternity in a real place called hell?

REWIND

Read Job 14:1–2, 10. For you, is death the end or a beginning? Explain your response.

_____

_____

_____

_____

_____

Death isn't the end; it is the beginning of a new life with God that will last forever. The promise of eternity in heaven can sustain us through life's problems, challenges, and disappointments.

Read 1 Corinthians 2:9–10. Rewrite these verses in your own words, expressing to God your feelings about His promise of heaven as your eternal destination.

_____

_____

_____

_____

_____

It's easy to get so focused on the present that we ignore the promise of the future. Yet our lives are full of chores that lead to future pleasure.

What are some of the chores you do on a regular basis that produce enjoyable results?

_____

_____

_____

_____

How do you stay motivated to perform these tasks?

_____

_____

_____

_____

The motivation for performing difficult chores often is the realization of the payoff. In struggling through school, you might have reminded yourself of the long-term value of the education. In going through a painful recuperation, you might have been reminded of the pain-free existence that waited on the other side. In living our lives, we must constantly be reminded of the perfect existence that awaits us in heaven. The reward is well worth the wait, and while we wait, we can do everything possible to encourage others to make the decision to accept God's offer of salvation. If we're going to spend eternity in heaven, let's take as many people as we can with us!

JOURNEY THROUGH GOD'S WORD

In the Christian vocabulary, *heaven* is a common word, but there is much confusion as to what and where heaven really is. In the broad sense, heaven is the place that serves as home for God and all heavenly beings.

The Old Testament writers didn't see a separation between God's dwelling and the earth; everything is a part of heaven. Heaven is the physical source for rain (Deuteronomy 11:11), dew (Genesis 27:28), frost (Job 38:29), snow (Isaiah 55:10), lightning (Genesis 19:24), dust (Deuteronomy 28:24), and hail (Joshua 10:11). Heaven is where God keeps the rain (Deuteronomy 28:12), wind (Jeremiah 10:13), and snow and hail (Job 38:22). Manna came from heaven when Israel was on the journey from Egypt to Canaan (Exodus 16:11–15).

In addition to being a place from which physical elements come, heaven plays a role in declaring God's glory

(Psalm 19:1) and righteousness (Psalm 50:6). People who did not know Yahweh God declared the heavens to be gods. This was the root of the Canaanite idol worship.

In the New Testament, heaven also is described as being above the earth, but there is no specific description of its exact location. In Acts 4:24, Luke declared that God created heaven. Matthew 11:25 says that heaven and earth are under God's control. Matthew 6:9 describes heaven as God's place of residence.

Jesus announced that heaven had come to earth in the form of His earthly ministry (Mark 1:15). According to Luke 10:20, those who believe in the Lord Jesus Christ have their names permanently recorded in heaven. Jesus went on to promise eternity in heaven to those who trusted in Him as Savior (John 14:2–3). Paul said that Jesus is seated next to God in heaven (2 Corinthians 5:1–2).

Heaven appears in the book of Revelation more than it does in any other book of the New Testament. In Revelation 21:1–22:5, heaven is described as:

1. The tabernacle (21:1–8)

2. The city (21:9–27)

3. The garden (22:1–5)[2]

> The conclusion is that the Bible portrays heaven as a real place where God's presence is supreme. Because of His love for us, we have the opportunity to join Him in that perfect place.

RETHINK

Describe what you think heaven will be like.

_____

_____

_____

_____

Our understanding of heaven is limited by our vocabulary, and we know that our vocabulary is inadequate to describe everything that heaven is. Jesus' disciples wondered what heaven would be like. In John 14:5, Thomas expressed their confusion over Jesus' destination when He left the earth.

Read the following Scriptures and list what each says about heaven.

Deuteronomy 26:15

_____

_____

_____

Revelation 21:11

_____

_____

_____

Revelation 21:21

_____

_____

_____

We can get caught up in describing what heaven will look like. It's more important, however, to understand what heaven will be like. There is only one alternative to spending eternity in heaven with God—that is spending eternity separated from God in a real place called hell.

There are also a lot of misconceptions about hell. Maybe you've heard someone say, "I don't mind going to hell because that's where all my friends will be." Nothing in Scripture suggests that hell will be a gathering place. Instead, hell will be a place of isolation from God and each other. It is described as a place of eternal fire and punishment. It is nothing to be desired or joked about.

Why would someone willingly choose hell over heaven?

_____ **Because they misunderstand hell.**

_____ **Because they misunderstand heaven.**

_____ **Because they misunderstand God.**

_____ **All of the above.**

How would you respond to someone who declared their comfort with spending eternity in hell?

_____

_____

_____

_____

_____

> *Never forget: Death was Satan's greatest victory. But by His death and resurrection, Jesus Christ reversed this. Think of it: Satan's greatest victory has now been turned into defeat! Death has now been put to death! Christ's motive in coming to earth was love, and His goal was to destroy death and take us to be with the Father forever. Jesus' resurrection proves beyond all doubt that death is not the end, and ahead of us is heaven.*
>
> BILLY GRAHAM
> *The Journey*

REFLECT

When Paul spoke of heaven, he spoke with certainty. He said "when," not "if." How did he know that heaven was real and that he would get to go there? He had never seen heaven or spoken with anyone who could describe it to him. Yet he declared that, "Our citizenship is in heaven. And we eagerly await a Savior from there, the Lord Jesus Christ . . ." (Philippians 3:20).

Citizenship carries both privileges and responsibilities. As a citizen, you have the right to vote, live with freedom and protection, work, and so forth. Along with those rights come responsibilities . . . paying taxes, respecting the rights of others, and so forth.

What might be some of the privileges of citizenship in heaven?

_____

_____

_____

_____

_____

What might be some of the responsibilities of citizenship in heaven?

_____

_____

_____

_____

Review the lists you just made. Are you more aware of the privileges or the responsibilities associated with citizenship in heaven? Why?

_____

_____

_____

_____

Paul knew two things—Jesus went to heaven following His earthly ministry, and Paul would get to go to heaven following his time on earth. The promise of heaven was something that motivated Paul to withstand the trials of life.

Think about your life. What are some of the trials you face?

_____

_____

_____

_____

How can the assurance of eternity in heaven help you face the trials you listed above?

_____

_____

_____

_____

We spend a lot of time trying to make our problems go away, only to discover that they are still with us. From self-help to self-destructive habits, people seem determined to try everything possible to escape the trials of life.

Read 2 Corinthians 11:22–27. List some of the dangers Paul faced while serving God.

_____

_____

_____

Now review the list above and circle all of the things Paul faced that you also have faced.

Chances are that you and I haven't faced what Paul faced. Our efforts to fulfill our callings in life haven't included the obstacles Paul encountered. Paul had every reason to give up and return to his old way of life, but he didn't. Paul's calling was stronger than any obstacle he faced.

What are some things that happen on a daily basis that interfere with your ability to stay focused on the promise of eternity in heaven with Jesus Christ?

_____

_____

_____

List three things you can do in order to remember God's promise of heaven even in the midst of trials and difficult situations.

1. _____

   _____

2. _____

   _____

3. _____

   _____

In Ephesians 2:19–22, Paul expressed to the Ephesian Christians that they were citizens of God's household. Let's take a closer look at this passage. Salvation brings about permanent changes in a person's life.

1. **We become members of God's household** (v. 19).
   Becoming a member of God's household means that we take on the characteristics of His children. We gain residency in His home—heaven—and we gain access to God. Being a child of God makes us His heirs.

Consider what it means to be an heir. What have you inherited from God?

_____

_____

_____

2. We gain a partnership with the giants of the faith who have preceded us (v. 20).

The apostles and prophets have helped lay the foundation upon which you and I now stand. Likewise, we contribute to the foundation upon which future generations will stand. In other words, we play an important part in the advancement of God's kingdom.

What are you doing to lay a strong spiritual foundation for future generations?

_____

_____

_____

3. **We become the temple of God** (vv. 21–22).

   When we become children of God, He comes to live in our lives. We can't go anywhere to escape His presence. We take Him everywhere we go. We show Him in everything we do.

What is your response to God's constant presence in your life?

_____ Uh-oh!

_____ I need to explain some things.

_____ I am glad He's with me.

REACT

When people pass away, we often refer to their graves as their final resting place. Yet, that description is more of a comfort than a reality. The grave isn't the end; there's more! If you know Jesus Christ as your Lord and Savior, you have the certainty that you will go to be with Him in heaven forever.

Read 1 Corinthians 15:51–58. What does this passage say to you about death?

_____

_____

_____

_____

Who are the people you know who need to hear about God's message of salvation?

_____

_____

_____

_____

Death is inevitable for all of us. Humanity's efforts to prolong life or avoid death always will be overshadowed by one fact—we will die! The question is, "What then?" What happens when this life is over? The Bible tells us that the choice we made while alive determines the place we spend eternity.

You already have made a choice. If you haven't chosen to accept God's gift of eternal life, you have decided to spend eternity in hell separated from God—you have made a tragic choice. Reconsider where you stand with God right now, and make sure you know that you will spend eternity with Him in heaven.

> *In heaven we will be with God. Think of it: We will be with God forever! We will be absolutely safe. Sorrow and suffering will never again touch us—never.*
>
> BILLY GRAHAM
> *The Journey*

What are three truths you learned in this study, and how will you apply each truth to your daily life?

1. _____

_____

_____

_____

2. _____

_____

_____

_____

3. _____

_____

_____

_____

6

Home
at
Last

T O GET THE MOST FROM THIS STUDY GUIDE, READ
pages 303–309 of *The Journey*.

*The Bible says this world is not our final home—but
we do have one, and that is heaven. Home is a place
of peace and joy—and so is heaven. Home is a place of
love and security—and so is heaven. Home is a place
of welcome and rest—and so is heaven.*

BILLY GRAHAM
The Journey

THINK ABOUT IT

*This world is the land of the dying; the next is the land of
the living.*

—TRYON EDWARDS[1]

Now we see but a poor reflection as in a mirror; then we shall see face to face. Now I know in part; then I shall know fully, even as I am fully known.

—1 Corinthians 13:12

There's a lot we don't know about heaven. Our minds can't comprehend its beauty or its size. We can't understand how it can be occupied by all of the saints yet seem so personal. We can only describe it in terms we understand—and those terms are inadequate.

What do you expect heaven to be? What will you do there? Those are great questions that deserve consideration. We know that heaven is reserved for those who have accepted Jesus Christ as Savior and Lord; there's no other way to get in.

REWIND

What are some things people do in order to "earn" a place in heaven?

_____

_____

_____

Can any of these actions secure a place in heaven? Why or why not?

_____

_____

_____

What must someone do to gain access to heaven?

_____ Sing in the choir

_____ Tithe

_____ Be a good person

_____ Attend church regularly

_____ Trust Jesus Christ as Lord and Savior

_____ Other: _____

The concept of the afterlife isn't new. Many ancient civilizations included ideas related to what happens when this life is over. Some people went to extremes to construct final resting places. The Egyptian pyramids are an example of this line of thinking. Into a pagan culture came the idea that God lived in heaven and desired His creation to spend eternity there with Him.

But what happens when someone dies? Is a person really "laid to rest," or is there something else that takes place? The Bible teaches that humans are made up of their physical natures and their spiritual natures. At death, the two natures are separated. The physical body is handled through earthly means, and the spiritual nature receives spiritual treatment.

Are you more concerned about the physical arrangements surrounding your death or the spiritual arrangements? Explain your response.

_____

_____

_____

Today many people prearrange their funerals. They purchase final resting places, select clothing, caskets, and pallbearers. They provide instructions regarding music and flowers. Yet many of these people who pay close attention to the physical details surrounding their death pay no attention to the spiritual aspects of life and death.

JOURNEY THROUGH GOD'S WORD

A survey of Egyptian culture is incomplete without a discussion of the pyramids. There are several examples of pyramids in Egypt, but the most famous are those built at Giza around 2500 BC. These pyramids that are among the Seven Wonders of the World.

The largest of the pyramids (known as the Great Pyramid) is 481 feet tall and 755 feet wide at the base. It was constructed under the leadership of Cheops around 2580 BC. His son and grandson were instrumental in the building of smaller pyramids near the Great Pyramid.

The pyramids served as burial places for and monuments to the rulers who had them built.

Because life in Egypt was tied to the fertile Nile delta, the Egyptians were optimistic in life and in death. Success in the land often resulted in aggressive building campaigns. The Israelites became slave laborers who assisted with some of the building that was taking place in Egypt.

Though architecturally impressive, the pyramids are nothing compared to the magnificence of heaven. Jesus was never impressed with the physical buildings of His time. He chose, instead, to remind people that physical structures are subject to the same forces that wear down the physical body.

> When it comes to the end of your life, will you be known for the "pyramid" you left as a reminder of your existence, or will you be known for the difference you made in the lives of people you met along life's journey?

RETHINK

Why is it so difficult for people to grasp the idea that heaven is a real place?

_____

_____

_____

We tend to believe only those things we can verify with our senses. We believe it is raining when we see, hear, or feel the rain. We believe a news story when we see the video. We believe our team won when we see the game. Heaven, however, can't be seen, heard, or touched. We can't experience real "heaven on earth" because we don't understand what heaven will really be like.

Before we consider what will happen to us when we get to heaven, we must make sure that heaven is really our eternal destination.

How do you know you will go to heaven when you die?

_____

_____

_____

If you said anything other than "because I have asked Jesus Christ to forgive me of my sins and to be my Savior and Lord," your admission to heaven might not be certain. Take a few moments right now and reconsider your relationship with Jesus Christ, and ask Him to come into your life.

The Bible doesn't answer all our questions about heaven and what it will be like—because heaven is far more glorious than anything we can imagine. Heaven is like the most perfect and beautiful place we can conceive—only more so. Only in heaven will we know exactly what heaven is like. Nevertheless, the Bible doesn't leave us in the dark about heaven—and everything it tells us should make us want to go there.

BILLY GRAHAM
The Journey

REFLECT

There are four truths the Bible says about heaven that we need to consider.

1. **In heaven, we will be with God.**
   The Bible teaches that God lives in heaven.

   Based on our relationship with Christ, we get to live where He lives. This might be confusing because we have been taught that God is everywhere. That's true, but before the earth came into being, God was in existence in the place called heaven.

Read 1 Thessalonians 4:17. How does Paul describe heaven?

_____

_____

_____

_____

Heaven is the place where there will be no more evil, sorrow, suffering, pain, illness, or problems.

Read Revelation 21:3–4. What are the characteristics of heaven described in this passage?

_____

_____

_____

_____

2. In heaven, we will be home.

Home can be a place of peace and joy. For some, it is a place of turmoil and unrest.

What or where is "home" to you?

_____

_____

_____

_____

Read Hebrews 11:13 and Philippians 3:20. Where is our real home?

_____

_____

_____

_____

_____

When we die, we enter into God's rest . . . provided we meet one condition—that we know Jesus Christ as Savior and Lord. Heaven won't be a place of boredom because we will be in God's presence at all times. We will worship God and reign with Him (Revelation 22:3, 5).

3. **In heaven, we will be like Christ.**
   This might be the most amazing aspect of heaven. While we live on this earth, we are challenged to become more and more like Christ. We can draw great encouragement from the fact that one day that transformation will be complete.

Read 1 Corinthians 15:51–52. What will this final transformation mean to you?

_____

_____

_____

_____

_____

As a result of this transformation, we will have new bodies. After His resurrection, Jesus' body was changed. There were no physical limitations; His body was perfect. This is the kind of body we all will have in heaven. The focus on the physical elements of life that are so prominent today will be gone. We don't know what we'll look like, but we will be changed.

In addition, our nature will be changed. Today, we are naturally sinners and pleasing God can be a struggle. Then, pleasing God will be natural and sinning will be impossible. How do we know this? Heaven is God's dwelling place where we will spend eternity in His presence, and God cannot be anywhere there is sin. So, if we are going to be in heaven, sin will be absent from us.

Read 1 John 3:2. Write this verse as a prayer of thanksgiving.

_____

_____

_____

4. **In heaven, we will be part of a new creation.**
   We live in a world in which everything is decaying. Our bodies show signs of age, and our natural resources are being depleted. But a time is coming when the perfection of the Garden of Eden will be restored and we will live in perfect harmony with God and our surroundings.

Read Romans 8:21 and Isaiah 11:6. What do these verses say about our future existence with God in heaven?

_____

_____

_____

When will all of this happen? It will happen when Jesus Christ returns to establish His authority over all creation. Can we predict the precise timing of Jesus' return? Contrary to some lines of thought, no!

Read 2 Peter 3:10–13. Based on this passage, when will Jesus Christ return?

_____

_____

_____

Based on the passage above, what will happen when Jesus returns?

_____

_____

_____

We have more information about what will happen than we do about when it will happen. When Jesus ascended into heaven, the angels promised that He would return someday (Acts 1:11).

Assume for a moment that some of the most intelligent schol-ars in the world gathered together and determined that Jesus

Christ would definitely return on a certain day in a certain year. The rumor of the timing of Christ's return travels quickly, and the countdown is on. Read Matthew 24:44. What does this verse say about the return of Christ?

_____

_____

_____

Why might someone hold to a human prediction in spite of God's declaration that no one knows when Jesus will return?

_____ Because people are smarter than God

_____ Because people choose to ignore parts of the Bible

_____ Because people don't want to know what the Bible says

_____ Because people want to believe they are in charge

_____ Other: _____

Whenever someone says he or she knows the timing of the return of Christ, you can be certain that person doesn't understand the truth of Scripture. Christ will return on God's schedule, not ours!

The joy that accompanies the return of Christ will be tempered by one truth—universal judgment.

Read Matthew 25:46. What will happen to people who reject God's offer of salvation?

_____

_____

_____

REACT

Ignoring God's coming judgment is a tragic mistake. Those people who are celebrated for their ungodly lifestyles and perversions of faith will stand before God and account for their actions. Not only will they account for their actions, but they also will have to stand responsible for all of those people they led astray. Worldly acceptance and popularity will be swallowed up in God's perfect judgment.

The bad news is that hell is real. The good news is that you don't have to go there. The vilest person in the world has the opportunity to turn from his or her ways and accept Jesus Christ as Savior and Lord.

Read Romans 8:1. List all of the people this verse excludes.

_____

_____

_____

What does the reality of heaven mean to us today? Pages 308–309 of _The Journey_ list these facts:

1. Because heaven is real, we have hope (Hebrews 6:19).

2. Because heaven is real, our lives have meaning and purpose.

3. Because heaven is real, we should live every moment for Christ (2 Peter 3:11–12).

Read 2 Corinthians 4:16–18 and then rewrite it in the first person. For instance, "Therefore, I do not lose heart . . ."

_____

_____

_____

Read your paraphrase of the passage above. How can you
make this passage a reality in your life today?

_____

_____

_____

_____

_____

_____

_____

*Don't let the burdens and hardships of this life dis-
tract you or discourage you, but keep your eyes firmly
fixed on what God has promised at the end of our
journey: heaven itself. Praise God for the hope we
have in Christ!*

BILLY GRAHAM
The Journey

What are three truths you learned in this study, and how will you apply each truth to your daily life?

1. _____

_____

_____

_____

2. _____

_____

_____

_____

3. _____

_____

_____

_____

NOTES

CHAPTER 1

1. Bob Kelly, *Worth Repeating*, 2003. Grand Rapids, MI: Kregel Publications, 117.
2. *Holman Illustrated Bible Dictionary*, 2003. Nashville, TN: B & H, 556–558.

CHAPTER 2

1. Bob Kelly, *Worth Repeating*, 9.
2. *Holman Illustrated Bible Dictionary*, 1039.

CHAPTER 3

1. Bob Kelly, *Worth Repeating*, 16.
2. *Holman Illustrated Bible Dictionary*, 1448–1449.

CHAPTER 4

1. Bob Kelly, *Worth Repeating*, 299.
2. *Holman Illustrated Bible Dictionary*, 297–298.

CHAPTER 5

1. Bob Kelly, *Worth Repeating*, 167.
2. *Holman Illustrated Bible Dictionary*, 732–734.

CHAPTER 6

1. Bob Kelly, *Worth Repeating*, 78.

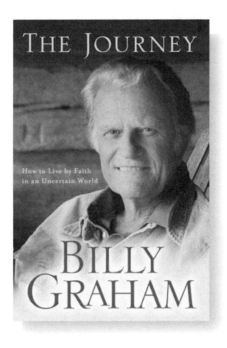

Billy Graham is respected and loved around the world.
The Journey is his magnum opus, the culmination of a
lifetime of experience and ministry. With insight that comes
only from a life spent with God, this book is filled with
wisdom, encouragement, hope, and inspiration for anyone
who wants to live a happier, more fulfilling life.

978-0-8499-1887-2 (PB)

STUDY GUIDE NOTES

_____
_____
_____
_____
_____
_____
_____
_____
_____
_____
_____
_____
_____
_____
_____
_____
_____
_____
_____
_____
_____
_____
_____

STUDY GUIDE NOTES

STUDY GUIDE NOTES